PENGUIN BOOKS

INSTALLATIONS

Joe Bonomo was born and raised in suburban Washington, D.C. He is also the author of *Sweat: The Story of the Fleshtones, America's Garage Band*. His personal essays and prose poems have appeared in numerous print and online journals and magazines. The recipient of fellowship awards in both prose and poetry from the Illinois Arts Council, he lives in DeKalb, Illinois, and teaches at Northern Illinois University.

The National Poetry Series was established in 1978 to ensure the publication of five poetry books annually through five participating publishers. Publication is funded by the Lannan Foundation; Stephen Graham; Joyce & Seward Johnson Foundation; Glenn and Renee Schaeffer; Juliet Lea Hillman Simonds Foundation; Tiny Tiger Foundation; and Charles B. Wright III.

2007 COMPETITION WINNERS

Joe Bonomo of DeKalb, Illinois, *Installations*
Chosen by Naomi Shihab Nye, to be published by Penguin Books

Oni Buchanan of Brighton, Massachusetts, *Spring*
Chosen by Mark Doty, to be published by University of Illinois Press

Sabra Loomis of New York, New York, *House Held Together by Winds*
Chosen by James Tate, to be published by HarperCollins Publishers

Donna Stonecipher of Berlin, Germany, *The Cosmopolitan*
Chosen by John Yau, to be published by Coffee House Press

Rodrigo Toscano of Brooklyn, New York, *Collapsible Poetics Theater*
Chosen by Marjorie Welish, to be published by Fence Books

INSTALLATIONS

Joe Bonomo

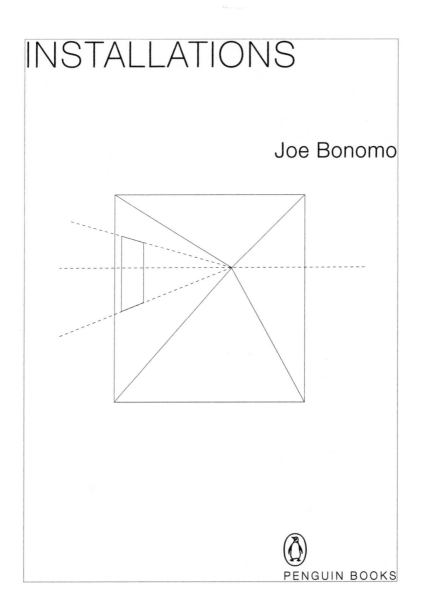

PENGUIN BOOKS

PENGUIN BOOKS

Published by the Penguin Group
Penguin Group (USA) Inc., 375 Hudson Street, New York, New York 10014, U.S.A.
Penguin Group (Canada), 90 Eglinton Avenue East, Suite 700, Toronto, Ontario, Canada M4P
2Y3 (a division of Pearson Penguin Canada Inc.)
Penguin Books Ltd, 80 Strand, London WC2R 0RL, England
Penguin Ireland, 25 St Stephen's Green, Dublin 2, Ireland (a division of Penguin Books Ltd)
Penguin Group (Australia), 250 Camberwell Road, Camberwell, Victoria 3124, Australia
(a division of Pearson Australia Group Pty Ltd)
Penguin Books India Pvt Ltd, 11 Community Centre, Panchsheel Park, New Delhi – 110 017,
India
Penguin Group (NZ), 67 Apollo Drive, Rosedale, North Shore 0632, New Zealand (a division of
Pearson New Zealand Ltd)
Penguin Books (South Africa) (Pty) Ltd, 24 Sturdee Avenue, Rosebank, Johannesburg 2196,
South Africa

Penguin Books Ltd, Registered Offices:
80 Strand, London WC2R 0RL, England

First published in Penguin Books 2008

10 9 8 7 6 5 4 3 2 1

Copyright © Joe Bonomo, 2008
All rights reserved

Page ix constitutes an extension of this copyright page.

LIBRARY OF CONGRESS CATALOGING IN PUBLICATION DATA
Bonomo, Joe, 1966–
Installations / Joe Bonomo.
p.   cm.—(National poetry series)
ISBN 978-0-14-311395-9
1. Installations (Art)—Poetry.   I. Title.
PS3552.O6375I5   2008
811'.54—dc22   2008009768

Printed in the United States of America
Set in Photina
Designed by Ginger Legato

For Amy

ONLY SILENCE PERFECTS SILENCE.

—A. R. AMMONS

ACKNOWLEDGMENTS

I am grateful to the editors at the following journals, where these pieces (indicated by their end lines) first appeared:

American Letters & Commentary ("And the installation will close." "Your body, in mourning and with great reluctance, received you back.")

Bayou ("You watch both bowls in the quiet humming of the room.")

Colorado Review ("Planes and birds glide in eternal gravity." In different form.)

Denver Quarterly ("And the book." "Were you to stand . . .")

In Posse Review ("For days afterward, you speak . . ." "6:47" "Spectators are encouraged to lie . . ." "The street's uniformity makes it impossible.")

The Laurel Review ("No one, you notice, has erased a line." "The exterior indistinguishable.")

Seneca Review ("You want to open that drawer.")

Sentence ("No one visits anymore.")

CONTENTS

Eventually your hands disappear entirely, vanish as they hover over the block letters, which, you now can see, you've arranged into a word. ▪ 46

☐

And again a voice asks, *What is that small bloom of dread in your chest that you can't name?* ▪ 51

You want to open that drawer. ▪ 53

You wish that the book were titled *Empathy* in a language that you knew. ▪ 57

Muttering complaints and a barely audible yes, you turn to go back in and toss the lighted cigarette that had suddenly appeared in your fingers and rub your eyes at the horses and buggies, the wet mud, the trolley cars. ▪ 59

If you step across you will vanish. ▪ 61

INSTALLATIONS

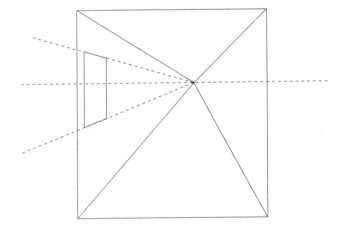

☐

A large, well-lit, white-walled room. You walk to a red line painted on the floor.

An eight-by-eight-foot wooden box, twelve inches deep, sits in the center of the room.

Gazing upward, you notice an enormous cutout hole, nearly the size of the ceiling itself. Clouds drift, far, far away. A bright black bird darts by.

Fortunately the weather is nice. Since this installation opened, the weather has been dry and mild.

The box is filled with eight inches of rich, dark soil. You reach your hand toward the soil. Your hand comes back wet. The soil looks fecund, nearly obscenely so.

You peer into the box and notice three human-size lumps. *These are human beings,* you think, *lying under the soil.* You look closer, assume that the lumps are static. But you notice the figures— barely perceptibly, as if in muted conversation—gesturing toward each other. One head nods gently toward another head; as if in a dream a mouth moves. The soil, though moist, is caked tightly, securing the figures snugly in a home of brown.

You lean in. The words are impossible. The words are muffled (of course!) but that's not the problem. You hear whole words, sentences, exclamations. Guttural sounds, lyric sounds, sounds of crying and sounds of ardor from dark currents in soil.

And if it were to rain? To where would the conversation be swept?

Above, the sun dips behind clouds and a brief shadow of abeyance sweeps gracefully across the three figures. You stand and stare, listening to their conversation, a conversation you swear later— tearing the program into tiny strips—never occurred. You exit the installation. You feel you have entered the world.

For days afterward, you speak in a strange tongue of loam and beetle, darkness and cake, root and worm.

☐

A large, well-lit, white-walled room. You walk to a red line painted on the floor.

Two shiny disks hang suspended from the ceiling on gray cords. You approach the disks, noting with pleasure that they are eye level. The room is quiet.

The disk on the left appears to be a clock, with a white face, large neatly painted numbers, elegant sweeping hands. The clock reads "4:43." (You wonder absently when the installation closes.)

The disk is slowly spinning clockwise. As the rear of the disk appears, you notice that the back of the clock has been removed. The clock's machinery—its metallic innards—is displayed. For the several moments that the back faces you before it rotates from view, you admire the clean efficiency, the flat humming workings, the precision, the *know-how*.

The clock face slowly rotates into view: "4:45."

You walk toward the other disk. It, too, revolves slowly but in a counterclockwise motion. The clock face is absent. In fact, this disk does not appear to be a clock at all. In place of numbers and hands, the word *ARTIFICE* is printed in large, black block letters.

The back has been removed from this disk also. There is nothing behind the disk. Empty. A void suspended.

You step back and watch both disks spin. The room hums in the quiet.

You look at the left disk.

"6:47."

□

A large, well-lit, white-walled room. You walk to a red line painted on the floor.

In the center of the room sits a large wading pool. A single mallard bobs in the water. Also floating are two television sets, both resting on bright green disks.

On one TV runs a loop of jet airliners taking off and landing. On the other TV runs a loop of birds and geese in flight. Both videos are silent.

As the absolute straight line does not yet exist in nature, the two inventions float on the surface of the water in formless semicircles. Often the mallard's wading direction is interrupted by the cord running from either TV to the outlet on a far wall. He renavigates.

The pool water is very still. The images on the screens are perpetual, the silence endless. The images are grainy, though fully representational.

The mallard is cute.

(Is there a fear of electrocution? Is there a vehicle for concern? The water seems clean enough, the room well tended.)

There is a thin strip of a window running along the cornice at the ceiling. Light bends in. Sometimes the TV screens float away, only to return. Sometimes the TV sets bump into each other or get stuck. The mallard is only slightly more graceful.

The scene is restive, if untranslated. Though implicated, you feel detached. Later you will climb into your car and drive back toward the city, away from this. For now you will try to feed, dig deep down into your pocket and wait.

The mallard dips its head beneath the surface.

On the televisions there are never-ending languages drifting toward some new hunger.

Planes and birds glide in eternal gravity.

☐

A large, well-lit, white-walled room. You walk to a red line painted on the floor.

In the center of the room, a film projector rests upon a simple wooden table. The projector is missing its rear spool. A book rests behind the projector on a tiny table.

Is it a novel? It's large enough to be a novel. It's a hardcover. Is it nonfiction? Poetry?

A continuous reel of film is thread from a slit in the book's cover onto the front spool. You look closer and notice that the film is actually a two-inch-wide continuous strip of the book's pages—there is discernible type on the strip, and the strip is clearly paper, not celluloid.

Quietly, endlessly, the strip unspools from the book into the projector, which spins its one reel.

A small screen is set up, twelve feet across the room from the projector. On the screen an image is projected. You walk toward the screen. You watch the screen and see an endless, grainy black-and-white loop of three consecutive images: a close-up of a man weeping in anguish for several seconds; another, different man wiping his hands together several times and then departing the frame; an aerial view of a dead-end street, without evidence of people, cars, living.

The small film repeats itself endlessly. And the book.

□

A large, well-lit, white-walled room. You walk to a red line painted on the floor.

In the center of the room two television sets sit on black metal stands. The stands face each other, approximately ten feet apart.

On each television screen plays a silent video loop.

On the left television screen, a young woman in a medium shot, nude but for a black thong, is standing and gently, slowly swaying her hips. She raises her hands and cups her breasts, fondles wide, erect nipples, runs both hands down her hips to suggestively touch and outline her thong. Every few moments she turns and sways her bottom for the camera, then turns back to resume her physical play. Her head is cut off by the top of the frame.

On the facing television set, an older woman in a medium shot, clothed in a housedress and apron, stands and gesticulates with her hands, as if she is talking to an unseen spectator. Every few moments she pauses to wipe her hands on her apron. Occasionally she folds her hands gently, once or twice places them nonthreateningly on her hips. Once—and then infinitely—she points directly at the camera. Her head is cut off by the top of the frame.

The room is quiet.

In between the two television sets there is a child-size bed in a wooden, Colonial-style frame, made up with a bedspread of indeterminate style and a down comforter. Lying on the bed is an eight-foot black whip, uncoiled, its thick handle resting on one of the two pillows.

Spectators are encouraged to lie on the bed and, if they disrupt the bedspread, to smooth it for the next visitor.

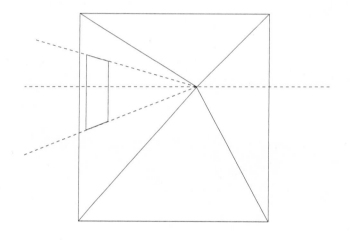

☐

A large, well-lit, white-walled room. You walk to a red line painted on the floor.

Two large treadmills sit in the center of the room, five feet apart. Each treadmill faces a television set that is mounted on an eight-foot metal stand. You observe that both treadmills are moving at "walking speed." One is moving forward, the other in reverse.

A small speaker is mounted on a metal post between the treadmills. The speaker broadcasts a loud, endless audio loop: an audience applauding; coins falling from one bucket into another bucket; a couple having noisy, enthusiastic sex; an audience laughing gratefully; more applause.

Both television sets project an endless video loop: the POV is from the middle of a wide, tree-lined avenue, gazing down a white dividing line that recedes with a gentle, lolling curve to the right at the vanishing point. Occasionally one or two people emerge from homes, stroll down the street. The image is restful, peaceful, in its way beautiful. The houses on the street are large and solid, the cars and accoutrement in the driveways and yards expensive, shiny, and newly purchased.

You notice, with not a little discomfort, that in the video mounted in front of the forward-moving treadmill, the camera pulls back endlessly, away from the suburban horizon.

You notice that in the video mounted in front of the backward-moving treadmill, the camera moves forward down the street, toward the endless suburban horizon.

You search for cords that plug the treadmills and speaker into the wall sockets. You can't find them.

Both video loops last several minutes. The street's uniformity makes it impossible to determine when the videos end and when they begin.

☐

A large, white-walled room. You walk to a red line painted on the floor.

In front of you, a heavy table made from dark gray Sheetrock. The room is dimly lit.

A disembodied voice utters, "In the beginning when God created the heavens and the earth, the earth was a formless void and darkness covered the face of the deep, . . ."

Intuitively you look up and around the room but cannot locate speakers.

Items are arranged on the table before you. To the far left lies a yellowing parchment. On the parchment is scrawled, "while a wind from God swept over the face of the waters. Then God said, 'Let there be light'; and there was light."

To the right of the parchment lies a large and heavily bound book, with paper as glossy as silk. On the open page, which is ornate with detailed and florid marginalia, is written, "And God saw that the light was good; and God separated the light from the darkness."

To the right of the book sits an envelope, shakily addressed. Gingerly you open the envelope, which is becoming gravely worn, and pull out a letter on thin paper. On the letter is written, "God called the light Day, and the darkness he called Night. And there was evening and there was morning, the first day."

To the right of the book sits a telegraph machine. It begins to click and chatter, as if being rattled by seismic activity. It clicks a staccato rhythm. Endlessly agitated, it clicks.

Next to the telegraph machine sits a heavy black Bakelite phone, circa early twentieth century. It rings abrasively. You pick it up, and listen. On the other end you hear, crackly, "And there was evening and there was morning, the first day." You can't place the voice, though it is oddly familiar.

To the right of the phone sits a bulky faux-paneled answering machine. Its red light blinks. Momentarily it emits a shrill beep. From the machine a disembodied voice intones, "And God said, 'Let there be a dome in the midst of the waters, and let it separate the waters from the waters.'"

The tape rewinds, resumes playing. The telegraph machine is tap-tapping. The phone rings again.

To the right of the answering machine lies a bright blue cell phone. It rings, playing "La Cucaracha." You pick up the phone and listen. On the other end you hear a distant voice that breaks up occasionally, "So God ma—— the dome and separ——ed the waters that ——under the dome from the ——ters that were ab——the dome. ——it was so."

You are the first spectator at the installation. You step back to watch and listen. The telegraph clicks and tap-taps and the phone rings and the answering machine beeps and the cell phone goes off again.

Soon the room is a cacophony of sound. You rush to answer the phone, and as soon as you hang it up it rings again.

You look wildly about you and notice that you are the only spectator. You cover your ears from the din and rush out.

A continent of noise.

No one visits anymore.

☐

A large, well-lit, white-walled room. You walk to a red line painted on the floor.

In front of you are two large easels, four feet apart. A canvas rests on each easel. A black rubber tube runs from a shallow tray at the bottom of each easel into a porcelain bowl placed on the floor. Next to the bowl are a single paintbrush and a sketch pad opened to a blank page.

On the left canvas a beautiful landscape has been painted, abstract yet representational, a haunting image of an expansive field with several large, dark trees randomly placed. The hues are shadowy and obscure, the trees dense with foliage, menacing and gorgeous in heavy and musical gloom. A treeless horizon blends into an early evening sky.

There are no people in the painting, only the private drama of landscape. You are moved by the power of the painting, the desolate grouping of arbitrary seed. You admire the painterly technique, the impasto, the thick, gestural textures.

On the right canvas a periodic table of the elements has been painted with designed precision in sharp, red and black hues. Group and subgroup, hydride and oxide, period and electron, lanthanide and actinide, number and weight—the chart is fierce and stunning in its exactitude and flawlessness. Your eyes drift over myriad symbols that swarm above you: Dy, Sn, As, Lr, Ru, Ni, Fr, Th, He, Li, La . . .

You rub your eyes.

All at once, an immense roar. Ducking and taking a step back, you manage to crane your head upward in time to see a sheet of water released from a long, thin metallic tube hanging twelve feet above the easels. The water falls in a pristine and immaculate sheet, as if a translucent curtain has dropped from the heavens.

The water crashes onto the canvases. You leap farther back but are sprayed.

The water has come in a dangerous, surprising burst, and quickly the room is filled with the sound of water dripping heavily from the canvases.

Cautiously, one eye trained on the tube above you, you approach the easels. The paintings are ruined, the canvases hopelessly stained, the compositions blurred and runny, barely recognizable.

Lamenting, you hear a tiny dripping sound at your feet, at first indistinguishable from the dripping off the easels. You look down and see that washed pigments have run down the tubes and have begun collecting in the bowl on the floor.

Tiny puddle of color.

A placard on the floor encourages you to pick up the brush, to dip it into the bowl, and to paint in the sketchbook.

You do so, making a hesitant, indeterminate line and swirl on the virginal page, and gaze upward, conscious of a looming and thunderous swell above your head.

☐

A large, well-lit, white-walled room. You walk to a red line painted on the floor.

Two medium-size porcelain bowls sit on the floor, two feet apart. Each bowl is filled with gray, cloudy water.

In the bowl on the left, the word *MEANING*, etched into a block of wood, floats on the surface of the water, drifting from one edge to the other.

In the bowl on the right, the surface is clear. The water appears undisturbed.

You watch both bowls in the quiet humming of the room.

Several minutes pass. In the bowl on the right, something stirs. You notice the word *MEANING* emerge from the shallow depths. It floats on the surface for a few moments, aimlessly from one edge of the bowl to the other, then submerges again, disappearing into the murky water.

After a minute, the word rises to the surface again. Within moments it resubmerges. This will continue.

In the bowl on the left, the word *MEANING* has drifted to the edge.

You watch both bowls in the quiet humming of the room.

□

A large, well-lit, white-walled room. You walk to a red line painted on the floor.

At the far left side of the room stands an easel. Propped on the easel is a writing pad. Hanging from the right end of the easel, on a cord, is a pencil. Hanging from the left end of the easel, on a cord, is a large pencil eraser.

At the installation's opening, the writing pad was turned to a large white sheet, empty but for an elemental drawing of two telephone poles, one at each end of the sheet.

Spectators were encouraged to approach the easel and, with pencil, draw a line from one telephone pole to the next.

Or to erase a line.

You have arrived at the installation late, harried and fearing the closing hour.

From a distance, the sheet of paper looks as if someone has violently attacked it with lead. As you approach, you see a tangle of thick, black lines, some precise and taut, others crudely, thickly drawn and loping. The two telephone poles are nearly hidden in the turmoil. The paper is torn in places. The easel has been jostled from its original position. The pencil has been worn down to a nub.

The eraser hangs, untouched, on its cord. No one, you notice, has erased a line.

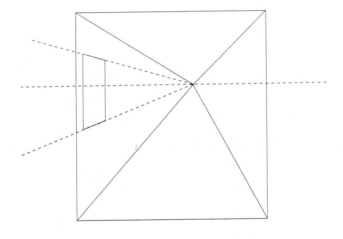

□

A large, well-lit, white-walled room. You walk to a red line painted on the floor.

Across the room stands a child's life-size playhouse. There is a doorway lacking a door and two windows, each lacking panes of glass, flanking the doorway. The roof is sloped and tiled conservatively.

On the left side of the house sits a gray metal industrial-size fan. Leaves fall from a large bag the color of a beige sky, hung a dozen or so feet above and slightly in front of the fan. Hundreds of leaves—fresh lime and moldy gold, burnt ruby and bright yellow— drop from the bag. The fan pushes them through the open window.

You peer into the window and watch as leaves blow in and slowly, determinedly, cover the toy kitchen table, the toy sofa, the toy ottoman, the toy coffee table, the toy bed.

The interior of the house is a bed of leaves. The exterior indistinguishable.

☐

A large, well-lit, white-walled room. You walk to a red line painted on the floor.

Just beyond the red line stands an easel. Resting on the easel is a white magnetized board. Randomly scattered across the board are large, black block letters:

CSRTOOATTGEEH

According to a plaque mounted into the floor, you and another spectator, a stranger, are instructed to rearrange the letters until they spell out a recognizable phrase.

You both stand in front of the easel, skeptical. You make the first hesitant move. You move an *E* in front of a *T*, an *R* after an *O*, an *S* all the way to the end of the phrase.

The letters remain inexplicable, obtuse.

The other spectator steps up, arranges and rearranges letters, frowns unhappily at the wash of incomprehension.

You both move letters across the board, trancelike, but the phrase remains unknowable. At times you feel as if you are approaching sense—or something recognizable—but meaning eludes you.

OTAOCTSGETREH

TOOACSTGEHERT

As you arrange and rearrange letters, you glance over at the other spectator. You are amazed. You were certain that she was a young woman, but this person next to you is clearly a man. What's more, the details of his face blur. His nose slides slowly across his face, his hair waves as if in a stiff breeze, his shoulders drop and rise like warm dough. He appears, as you both now arrange and rearrange letters in a kind of ecstatic fog, to rotate slowly or to drift or slide blade-thin across the room, vanishing into the corners and back again. And the letters move.

TOCSATTGOEHTRE

TOCASTTOGETHER

TOCASTTOGETHER

TOCASTTOGETHER

Triumphant, wholly shocked, you turn toward the spectator to share the victory. He is gone. That is, his details have evaporated. He is a silhouette, a ghost of a person through whom you could move your hand.

The easel has vanished, has become an intangible presence, a blurry silhouette in a room, a symbol for a lucid and evanescing presence.

☐

A large, well-lit, white-walled room. You walk to a red line painted on the floor.

A wooden box, three feet by three feet and two feet deep, is centered on a wooden table. A wooden lid has been screwed onto the top of the box.

You approach the table and the box and can see bright flickering inside, through thin gaps where the lid of the box meets the sides of the box.

You lean in closer. You hear sounds, contained, tiny, muffled. You cock an ear and can just make out noise of applause, of men and women talking, now a scream, now laughter, and now unintelligible mutterings of a conversation between what sounds like two people.

Flickering continues inside the box, bright, now muted, now bright again.

Just beneath the layer of audio you hear a consistent *tick-i-tick-i-tick-i-tick* . . .

A motion picture projector is running inside the box, projecting images and sounds that no one can see or hear.

Next to the box is another, smaller wooden box labeled on its side "Pens & Pencils."

The box is open and you see scattered inside various pens and pencils: felt-tip, ballpoint, freshly sharpened and short nubby pencils, markers of various sizes.

Scattered among the pens and pencils are half a dozen screwdrivers with various-colored handles.

According to a plaque on the floor, spectators are encouraged to use the screwdrivers to open the box.

You choose a screwdriver and turn to the box, eager to unscrew and lift the lid. The first screwdriver you choose is too small for the heavy-duty screws. You return and choose another screwdriver, which is also too small. Both screwdrivers are too tiny to use even as wedges to loosen the firmly tightened screws. You return to the box and discover to your dismay that the remaining screwdrivers are Phillips head, when what you need is a flat head.

The film continues to play in the dark, closed box.

□

A large, well-lit, white-walled room. You walk to a red line painted on the floor.

Two tables with white Formica tops. A tiny, black screw—less than a centimeter in length, so tiny as to be nearly invisible—rests in the center of the table to the left.

A tiny white wildflower—its bloom less than a centimeter in width, so tiny as to be nearly invisible—rests in the center of the table to the right.

The wildflower will, of course, eventually wither and die. And the installation will close.

☐

A large, well-lit, white-walled room. You walk to a red line painted on the floor.

A three-foot-high polyurethane wall stands five feet away from a window that lets warm, glowing light into the room. The dark gray wall casts a long shadow, in the middle of which a potted plant sits on the floor. Its single sprout has withered and is dry and near death.

On the floor, a few feet away from the plant, a ten-inch-high clock sits just past the end of the shadow cast by the wall.

You notice activity on the clock face behind the glass.

You look closer and notice that dozens of ants are scurrying to and fro over the clock face. They are trapped behind the glass and roam the face, apparently aimlessly, madly from number to number. Some ants run behind one side of the face, into the concealed workings of the clock, and reappear on the other side. You try following one ant, but it is hopeless to track his movement among the others.

The clock ticks, its red second hand sweeping smoothly above the ants, a metronome gliding above chaos.

Were you to stand at this installation for a lengthy period, you would notice the shadow cast by the wall lengthen slowly, nearing the clock with the day's precision.

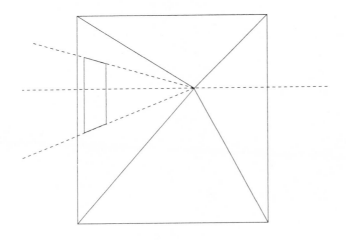

□

A large, well-lit, white-walled room. You walk to a red line painted on the floor.

Two screens, each roughly six by six feet, are mounted on two separate aluminum stands located three feet from the rear wall. A narrow strip of window runs along the cornice at the top of the wall, pouring a thin liquid of yellow light into the room. You notice dark bird shapes flitting past the window. Occasionally a passing cloud darkens the window.

Two continuously looping films run alternately on the screens.

On the left screen is a short film of stampeding buffalo, a high-angle shot that captures the herd thundering toward you from a placeless dusty horizon until the screen is filled with a roiling wave of brown and black muscled movement. The right screen is dark.

Presently on the right screen is a short film of a speeding train, moving, you intuit, east to west. The angle is ground level and captures only the middle cars; the engine and caboose remain unseen. The impression is of an endless train, fulminating, making the ground beneath it tremble in an infinite clamor. The left screen is now dark.

Mounted above each screen is a small speaker. When the film of the buffalo is projected, the sound of a roaring train bursts from the speaker. When the film of the train is projected, the sound of stampeding buffalo bursts from the speaker.

You only know this because you cheated, of course. Before you entered the room a small plaque mounted near the entrance requested that you shut your eyes for the duration of your visit. You had full intention to do so but before long felt an irresistible urge to open your eyes.

Your body, in mourning and with great reluctance, received you back.

☐

A large, well-lit, white-walled room. You walk to a red line painted on the floor.

In front of you on the floor is a neatly cut square of bright green Astroturf, roughly four feet by four feet.

In the precise center of the square of Astroturf sits a shiny metal robot from a 1950s sci-fi movie.

In front of the robot is a neatly wrapped Twinkie. An offering.

In front of the Twinkie a group of plastic Indians—in various poses of menace, defense, and fear—circles warily. A molded plastic buffalo and its young—a tableau you've seen for sale at truck stops—sit placidly in the corner of the Astroturf.

With history in front of you, you feel a tingle at the back of your neck, and you turn around.

☐

A large, well-lit, white-walled room. You walk to a red line painted on the floor.

On a long, low table before you sits a television set of a certain vintage. Its body is large, the screen oddly bulbous, the knobs (the knobs!) bulky. You notice a thin film of dust on the screen.

The set is broadcasting an old Tarzan film, circa early 1960s. Tarzan is standing on a low, broad tree branch, gesticulating and pointing offscreen through hazy sunlight. The actor is tan and possesses jet black molded hair, and he appears fit, although his tan looks artificial and he appears to be holding in his gut.

The scene cuts between an array of chattering jungle animals below Tarzan and Tarzan up on the branch, looking vaguely heroic. There is a certain urgency to the scene, you must admit.

But the colors look washed out, faded, as if tinted ash gray. This makes you sad. The images appear fuzzy, though you don't know whether that is the result of poor grainy film or the television set's vintage.

Next to the television sits a large window-unit air conditioner, angled to face the screen. A heavy utility cable connects the unit to a three-pronged outlet on the wall.

The air conditioner is set on high and blows ice-cold conditioned air onto the TV set. Under the table lies a cheap leopard-skin rug, in an oval shape.

☐

A large, well-lit, white-walled room. You walk to a red line painted on the floor.

You hear a buzz, a low thrumming in your sinuses.

Two potted trees stand at either end of the room. Their trunks taper elegantly, their bark looks healthy. Topping each tree is a burst of foliage, green felt Russian hats.

A thick, black telephone wire runs from one tree to the other tree. The wire is taut.

An arrow on the floor directs you to walk toward a pair of heavy-duty wire cutters, suspended from the ceiling on a cord with ample slack.

A placard nailed on the floor encourages you to lift the shears, to ascend a small ladder positioned in the center of the room, and to cut the wire.

You examine the trees again. They stand erect, but a small dread in your chest blooms and you intuit that the trees, falling gently each away from the other, are held aloft by the taut wire.

If you were to cut the wire, the trees would collapse and crash to the floor.

You scan the room stupidly, hoping to find a bird or three. How will they help your decision?

What is that small bloom of dread in your chest that you can't name?

□

A large, well-lit, white-walled room. You walk to a red line painted on the floor.

In front of you, on a large, wooden table, three block letters rest in a shallow box.

The letters are *T*, *R*, and *A*.

A placard in front of the box reads, "ar: to fit, to join together."

The spectator is encouraged to lift the three block letters from the shallow box and arrange them on the table to form a word or a sound or a song or a world.

You try to lift the block letters and are astonished at their weight. You must use both arms to lift a single block letter, this after leaning your entire body against the table for ballast and leverage.

Eventually you're able to remove each block letter. You drop each on the table with a loud and echoing *THUD*.

After a breather, you reach for the letters, intent on arranging them into a word, or a sound, or a song, or a world, and when your hand touches the blocks it metamorphoses into another's hand, a woman's, say, with long painted fingernails, or another man's hands, thick and spotted with rough-hewn nails. Several more attempts, and several more times your hands change shape in front of your disbelieving eyes: a small boy's hands, thin and bony; now a fury paw, pulsing along tendons; and now an old woman's, graceful as silk over ramshackle bone.

Eventually your hands disappear entirely, vanish as they hover over the block letters, which, you now can see, you've arranged into a word.

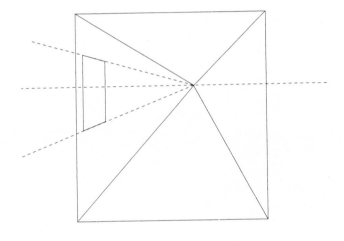

☐

A large, white-walled room. You walk to a red line painted on the floor.

The room is dimly lit. In front of you, a television set sits upended, its back on the floor. It is turned on. You don't know what program is playing, you think probably a sitcom, judging from the hoarse laughter.

A sheet of black felt covers the front of the set from end to end. The set flickers and light pours out from a myriad of pinholes pricked into the felt, projecting shapes onto the ceiling. You glance upward and see an astronomy of shifting, pretty light.

A few feet to the right of the television stands a small table, and on it a telescope pointed at the ceiling.

A foot to the right of the small table stands a lectern, and on it a wooden box with a hinged lid. The box is labeled "The Book of the Heavens."

You enjoy the quiet of the room, the muted humming from the television, the otherworldly specter of the light arranged as a universe of celestial heavens on the ceiling.

Trusting an impulse of fate, searching for meaning in your dark ceiling, you open the box labeled "The Book of the Heavens." Inside lies a recent issue of *TV Guide*.

And again a voice asks, *What is that small bloom of dread in your chest that you can't name?*

☐

A large, well-lit, white-walled room. You walk to a red line painted on the floor.

In the center of the room are three small wooden tables placed end to end.

On the left table sits a potted plant, a geranium you think. Four bright red blooms poke expectantly from dark soil. You think of four kids. The pot is wrapped carefully and festively in foil.

Next to the plant rests a book. Spectators are encouraged to approach the table and peruse the book. You do so, noting that it's a hardcover of an indeterminate age, the corners and edges softened. The book is a botanical text. You flip through, notice glossy photos of exotic-looking flowers, small print, dense text, musty odors. You place the book back on the table, and the pages fall open to an entry on geraniums.

You move to the middle table, on which sits a white iPod, its earbud cord resting in front of it like a thin, polished garden snake. Spectators are encouraged to listen to the music playing on the iPod. You do so, securing the left bud as it threatens to fall from your ear. You hear something symphonic, something orchestral playing, what sounds to you like a swell of classical music (*did I come in the middle?*), dramatic and purposeful. You couldn't name the music or the composer if you were asked. The music is pleasant and mournful, and alert and sad. You find yourself staring at your feet.

Next to the iPod rests a large stack of sheet music. You turn off the player, place the earbuds back on the table, rifle through the music. The score (*is that the correct term?*) looks mathematical, although there aren't any numbers. No, wait, there are. The score is mathematical, you note with mild interest. The composers' names look European. The pages appear old, of an other-century vintage. A small placard, affixed to the table with screws, encourages the spectators to read the sheet music while listening to the iPod. You have little interest in doing this.

You move to the right table, which is empty. Spectators are encouraged to imagine that the empty space is filled with anything they wish. You wish you had a program. *Why?* You wish you had your cell phone. *Why?* You wish the door behind you was larger. *Why?* You're hungry, though you just had lunch. *Why?* You wish that someone would tell you what's on the table.

You swear that the ceiling is higher.

The table has a small drawer. You hadn't noticed before. You are hesitant to open it, especially as there is no placard encouraging you to do so.

The table looks friendly, and that strikes you as odd. You lean toward it and notice, with your throat tightening, the various swirls and varnish strokes that create the rich, musical textures of the tabletop. You feel longing and yearning for the table, which also strikes you as odd. You wonder what tree, where, was felled to make this table, and how the tree was shorn and bundled and assembled. You imagine a bird's-eye view of the country, a red dot blinking to indicate the precise state, county, and township where the forest is. You wonder about the smells and sounds of the factory, the lives of the workers there. You think about opening the drawer.

You want to put your arm around this table; you want to take this table out, blinking, into the high sun and steer it toward the nearest dark bar and drink all night. You want to lean in and rub your arms along its smooth legs, its broad top, caress its round corners with light fingertips, raise a toast, but you know that the guard would yell.

You wonder how you can even leave the room. The door has vanished. The light leaning in through the high windows is in your head. There are no windows now, only a table with emptiness and a history that you would not find in a book.

The table is musical—the table is music—and the legs and edges blur and vanish. The borders of the table (*this essay, this poem*) disappear from you. Now in front of you is pure song. You know this but you cannot say this.

(*What am I supposed to do?*) You are calm and terrified. Although you are scared, you are refreshed. The table's song will sing you. You want to open that drawer.

□

A large, well-lit, white-walled room. You walk to a red line painted on the floor.

On the floor in front of you is a white chalk outline of a body. You feel, *This is very much like a crime scene*, and yet you don't shiver or look away.

There are several spectators with you. One walks to a low wood table near the red line and picks up a book. She leafs through it. Over her shoulder, you notice that the pages are empty.

She reads instructions printed on a placard nailed to the floor. She steps toward the chalk outline and kneels next to it. She opens the book she's holding to a random page of milk white.

To your astonishment she stretches her body out and fits herself into the chalk outline. The outline matches her body perfectly, top to bottom, side to side.

She stands, walks over to you, and hands you the book. You confirm, leafing through the volume, that the pages are blank. The cover is blank.

You step toward the chalk outline and, clutching the book awkwardly in one hand, sink to your knees and then stretch your body inside the outline. To your astonishment the outline fits you perfectly. You feel transported, held, refreshed.

You stand up and hand the book to another spectator, who kneels in the outline, stretches his body, and lies in a flawless match.

You pick up another book from the low table. You wish that the book had words, you wish that you could read and understand. You wish that the book were titled *Empathy* in a language that you knew.

□

A large, well-lit, white-walled room.

You pause at the door, thinking twice. Instead of entering, you turn and walk back down the hall, into the foyer, and out the front door.

Outside, you stand at the bottom of the steps, gazing at passing traffic that moves by in ghostly pulses. You're hesitant to go back in. You feel as if you're a blur, like you're in a transparent overlay where the second page is off a fraction. You remember when you were a kid and when spring would come, and on the first bright, really clear day the trees and buildings and people around you looked as if they were outlined in a thick, throbbing black line, humming as if a power line was wound tight around every-thing.

The street looks that way to you now. You find that you're absently tugging at the base of your neck, afraid that your head might un-hook and come off. You're scared and you vaguely remember read-ing about voodoo and magic, and now you remember Barry's Magic Shop in the old neighborhood, how your brothers would dart in and out on carefree weekends, coming home with tricks and gags, but you'd avoid the place, queasy in the lure to know how the tricks work, fearing the answers. Remember at the rec center when the magician bent over and his pants ripped and the flesh-covered thumb tip fell out of his pocket? You still mourn that long night under fluorescent lights.

You're afraid to go back in. You remember that Stevens said, "Reality is a cliché from which we escape by metaphor." Muttering complaints and a barely audible yes, you turn to go back in and toss the lighted cigarette that had suddenly appeared in your fingers and rub your eyes at the horses and buggies, the wet mud, the trolley cars.

□

A large, well-lit, white-walled room. You walk to a red line painted on the floor.

If you step across the red line you will vanish.

If you step across you will metamorphose.

If you step across you will articulate.

If you step across you will assemble.

If you step across you will arrange and rearrange.

If you step across you will not come back.

If you step across you will break.

If you step across you will mend.

If you step across you will be refreshed.

If you step across you might return refreshed.

If you step across you will learn to sing.

If you step across you will forget to speak.

If you step across you will be shaped and you will shape.

If you step across you will bear witness.

If you step across you will bear burden.

If you step across you will bear across.

If you step across you will transfer.

If you step across you will eliminate *like* or *as*.

If you step across you will awaken in the middle of a magic trick.

If you step across you will pregender.

If you step across you will become a child with an old man's heart.

If you step across you will become an old woman with a child's heart.
If you step across you will see inside.
If you step across you will fuse, and for the purposes of comparison you will become one.
If you step across you enter all books.
If you step across you enter all film.
If you step across you enter plastic and understand grief.
If you step across you will never grieve.
If you step across you will put it together.
If you step across you will become.
If you step across you will revise.
If you step across you will vanish.